Islamic Empires

600–1650

FOUNDATION

John D. Clare

Hodder Murray

A MEMBER OF THE HODDER HEADLINE GROUP

Acknowledgements

Cover photos show a portrait of Saladin courtesy of Uffizi Gallery Florence, SEF/Art Resource, NY, and The Charge of the Cavaliers of Faramouz, from a 'Shahnama' Persian School (14th century) courtesy of the Louvre, Paris, France/Bridgeman Art Library.

The publishers would like to thank the following individuals, institutions and companies for permission to reproduce copyright illustrations in this book:

© Yann Arthus-Bertrand/ CORBIS: p3; 033446 © Bildarchiv Steffens/ Henri Stierlin, sixteenth-century Istanbul, Topkapi Library, MS Sijer I-Nebi: p4 (left); ©.Peter Sanders: p4 (right); © Dean Conger/CORBIS: p6; © CORBIS: p7; British Library, Dept of Indian and Oriental Manuscripts, Battle on Camels MS 25900: p11; © Vittoriano Rastelli/CORBIS: p14; Institut Amatller D'Art Hispànic, El Escorial (Madrid), Monastère de San Lorenzo el Real, MS S.XIII: Cántigas de Santa María: p15; Biblioteque Nationale, MS Arabe 5367 F∞/18v9: p19; © Biblioteca Apostolica Vaticana/ AR 368 10: p23; Werner Forman Archive: p25 (left and right); Nasser D. Khalili Collection of Islamic Art, CAL 242: p26 (top); © Diego Lezama Orezzoli/CORBIS: p26 (bottom); Chester Beatty MS3 folio 143r, © The Trustees of the Chester Beatty Library, Dublin: p27 (bottom); The Metropolitan Museum of Art, Rogers Fund, 1918. (17.81.4) Photograph ©1986 The Metropolitan Museum of Art: p27 (top); XYL155434 FY 1404 Takyuddin and other astronomers at the Galata observatory founded in 1557 by Sultan Suleyman, from the Sehinsahname ofx by Turkish School (16th century) University Library, Istanbul, Turkey/ Bridgeman Art Library: p28; Bodleian Library, MS Fraser 201 folio 1041r: p29 (top); Bodleian Library, MS Pococke 375 folio 3v 4r: p29 (bottom); British Library, BL MS.Or.2780f. 61r: p31; Life File Photo Library/ Mike Evans: p32; Biblioteque Nationale, MS Fr5594 folio 213: p34; Institut Amatller D'Art Hispànic, El Escorial (Madrid) Monastère de San Lorenzo el Real. MS S.XIII: Livre des Jeux de Échecs: p37; The Metropolitan Museum of Art, Francis M. Weld Fund, 1950. (50.164) Photograph ©1977 The Metropolitan Museum of Art: p39 (left); © Archivo Iconografico, S.A./CORBIS: p39; Royal Armouries, Leeds: p40; Akhbarnama, Victoria & Albert Museum, London: p41; Life File Photo Library/ Gina Green: p42; Baburnama, Victoria & Albert Museum, London: p43 (top, left); Life File Photo Library/ Barry Mayes: p43 (bottom); 1978.2597 EA, Ashmolean Museum, Oxford: p43 (top, right); British Library, BL Add Or 1039: p44.

Every effort has been made to trace and acknowledge ownership of copyright. The publishers will be glad to make suitable arrangements with any copyright holders whom it has not been possible to contact.

Artworks and Illustrations by Barking Dog Art.
Layout by Janet McCallum.

Orders: please contact Bookpoint Ltd, 130 Milton Park, Abingdon, Oxon OX14 4SB. Telephone: (44) 01235 827720. Fax: (44) 01235 400454. Lines are open from 9.00 - 5.00, Monday to Saturday, with a 24-hour message answering service. You can also order through our website www.hoddereducation.co.uk.

British Library Cataloguing in Publication Data
A catalogue record for this title is available from the British Library

ISBN-10: 0-340-81199-4
ISBN-13: 978-0-340-81199-3

First Published 2004
Impression number   10 9 8 7 6 5 4 3
Year   2010 2009 2008 2007 2006

Printed in Italy for Hodder Education, a member of the Hodder Headline Group, 338 Euston Road, London NW1 3BH.

Contents

1 THE DAWN OF ISLAM

The Big Picture   2

Thinking it Through

Muhammad, the Messenger of God   4

The Qur'an and Hadith   6

Investigation

Who should succeed the Prophet?   8

2 THE EMPIRE UNFURLS 632–1000

The Big Picture   10

Thinking it Through

The conquest of Spain   12

What was Cordoba famous for?   14

Investigation

How free and mixed was Al-Andalus?   16

3 ISLAMIC CIVILISATION

The Big Picture   18

Thinking it Through

Social class   20

Investigation

The life of women   22

Thinking it Through

Cities, homes and gardens   24

Islamic arts   26

Investigation

Islamic science and technology   28

4 HOLY WARS 1000–1500

The Big Picture   30

Thinking it Through

Were the Crusades a Jihad?   32

How successful were the Crusades?   34

Investigation

Two commanders compared   36

5 NEW EMPIRES FOR OLD 1500–1650

The Big Picture   38

Thinking it Through

The Mughal Empire   40

What did the Mughals achieve?   42

Investigation

Survival skills for rulers   44

INDEX   46

1 THE DAWN OF ISLAM

IN THIS CHAPTER YOU WILL LEARN:

- What the world was like in 600.
- How Muhammad started Islam.
- What happened when Muhammad died.

The world before Islam

The great world religion of Islam started off with one man who lived in the desert in the Middle East.

Yet his followers conquered many countries in less than a hundred years. Many people find this amazing!

What was the world like in about 600?

a. Europe: lots of small weak countries. Always at war. France and Spain were quite rich and were Christian countries, but the people hated their rulers.

b. Constantinople: all that was left of the Roman Empire. Rich lands, but weak. Always at war with Persia. Christian.

NEW WORDS

Islam: the new religion started by Muhammad.

Constantinople

religion

conquered

follower

believe

Empire

Zoroastrians: the religion of Persia.

oasis: a watering hole.

meteorite: a lump of rock from outer space.

Kaaba: a building in Mecca, the most holy place of Islam.

idol: a statue which people worship.

peace

SOURCE A

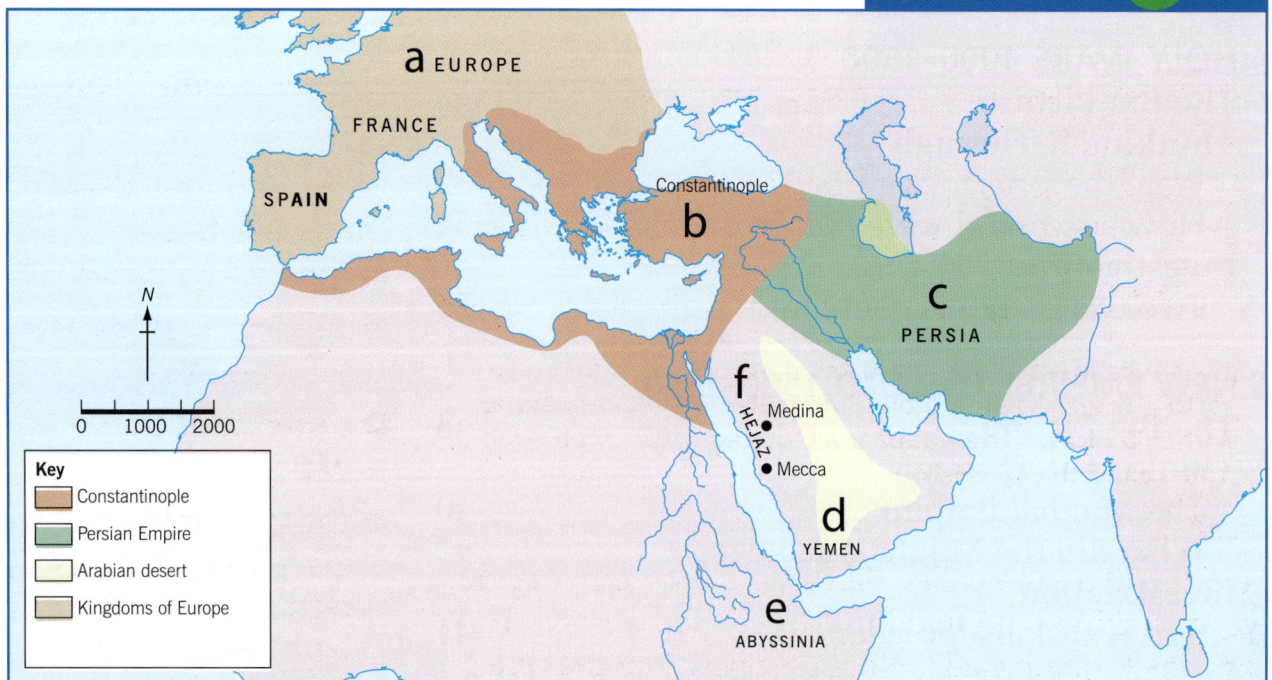

▲ *The Middle East about 600.*

Key
- Constantinople
- Persian Empire
- Arabian desert
- Kingdoms of Europe

SOURCE B

▲ The Hejaz was a poor desert place.

The word Islam comes from the Muslim way to say 'hello' – *asalam aleykum* – which means 'Peace be with you'.

SOURCE C

The Quraish tribe were very important among the Arab tribes because they looked after the Kaaba.

▲ Written by a modern historian.

c. **Persia:** a very rich empire, but quite weak. Always at war with Constantinople. The Persians were Zoroastrians, a religion which believed that a new good leader, sent from God, would come to the world in 628.

d. **Yemen:** quite rich farmland, but in 600 the Yemen was ruled by the Persian Empire. There was a mix of religions in the Yemen.

e. **Abyssinia:** small mountain kingdom in Africa. Quite rich. Christian.

f. **The Hejaz:** a desert, with now and again a water-hole (called an 'oasis'). The people were poor. The different tribes were always fighting.
    In 600 the people of the Hejaz had many different gods. They also believed that some places were holy. One holy place was Mecca, where a black meteorite had fallen to earth. It was kept in a building called the Kaaba, along with 360 idols. The Kaaba was looked after by an Arab tribe called the Quraish.

About 570 a man called Abdullah, a member of the Quraish tribe who lived in Mecca, had a son. This son was Muhammad. Nobody knew it at the time, but the boy was going to change the world!

Tasks

1. Find on the map: Europe, Constantinople, Persia, Yemen, Abyssinia and the Hejaz. For each, say:
● what religion,
● how rich, and
● how strong they were.

2. How might the following have helped Islam grow:
● other countries were weak,
● other countries were at war,
● the Zoroastrians were expecting a good man sent from God.

Muhammad, the Messenger of God

When Muhammad was six years old, his parents died and he had to live with his uncle, Abu Talib.

He looked after his uncle's sheep.   He grew up
5   to be a good and honest man.

The message

Abu Talib was a trader.   One day in 595 a rich widow named Khadija asked him if he knew of an honest man who could run her business.
10   That was how she met Muhammad, and soon after they were married.   She was more than 30 years old, he about 25.

Muslims believe that, about **610**, Muhammad began to get messages from an angel.   He was
15   told that there was only One God – Allah.   At first he kept quiet about this, but then he began to tell people.   Many people listened to him.

Muslims add the words 'Peace and blessings upon him' (usually just the letters pbuh) whenever they say or write Muhammad's name.

SOURCE A

▲ *An early Muslim drawing of the Kaaba.*

▲ *This photo shows modern Muslims at the Kaaba – every Muslim hopes to go to Mecca at least once in their life.*

SOURCE B

Muhammad's followers were not united by family – as the Arab tribes had been before – but by religion.

This was a new thing in Arabia – the Muslims were a new supertribe.

▲ *Written by a modern historian.*

SOURCE C

Do not argue with... Christians and Muslims except in the nicest possible manner ... and say, '...our god and your god is one'.

▲ *A quote from the Qur'an, Surah 29, The Spider, verse 46.*

SOURCE D

Everything changed for Muhammad when he went to Medina.

He became the boss. People did as he said.

The people of Mecca had attacked Islam; the people of Medina became Muslims.

▲ *Written by a modern historian.*

The Hijra

The leaders of the Quraish tribe did not like this new religion. They were afraid that people would stop going to Mecca to worship at the Kaaba. About the same time, both Khadija and Abu Talib died. [20]

Things became so bad that, in **622**, Muhammad and his followers had to flee from Mecca to the town of Medina, 280 miles away. This is called 'the Hijra'. Muslims date their calendar from this event. [25]

First Muslim successes [30]

By now, the followers of Muhammad were calling him 'the Prophet', and themselves 'Muslims'. They grew in numbers. They were good fighters. In **630** a large Muslim army marched to Mecca, captured it and destroyed all the idols. [35]

By the time Muhammad died in 632, Islam had become the religion of all Arabia.

Tasks

1. Prepare the grid for a timeline of events, 600–1700. Find the THREE dates in bold on pages 4–5, and mark the events on the timeline.

2. Work with a partner. Imagine that it is 632, and that a Muslim is asked these questions:

● How did the religion start?

● How is it different?

● How were you treated in Mecca?

● How successful is the new religion?

● Why is it so successful?

Prepare your answers and act out the interview.

The Qur'an and Hadith

The holy book of Islam is called the Qur'an.

It is very important to Muslims. Muslims believe that, when they read it, they are reading the words of God.

Structure of the Qur'an

The Qur'an is not a history book. It does not tell us about what happened. It has lots of religious sayings. It is made up of chapters called Surahs.

NEW WORDS

Qur'an: the Muslim holy book.

Surah: a chapter in the Qur'an.

memorise

according to

Hadith: stories about the life and sayings of Muhammad.

Respect

Muslims think every copy of the Qur'an is holy. They do not put it on the floor. They never put another book on top of it. In some countries, old copies of the Qur'an are kept in huge caves so they will not get thrown away.

Traditional stories

Muslim writers also wrote down the sayings and deeds of Muhammad. These are called hadith. They are not the words of Allah, but they are important to Muslims. They include stories from the history of Islam.

SOURCE A

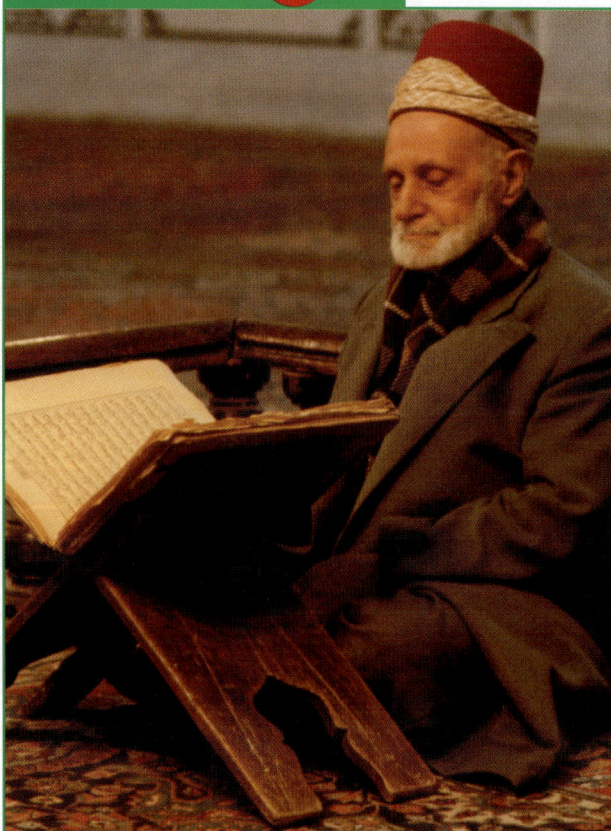

▲ *A Muslim reading the Qur'an.*

Muslim children try to memorise the 600 pages of the Qur'an in Arabic – even if they cannot understand Arabic.

SOURCE B

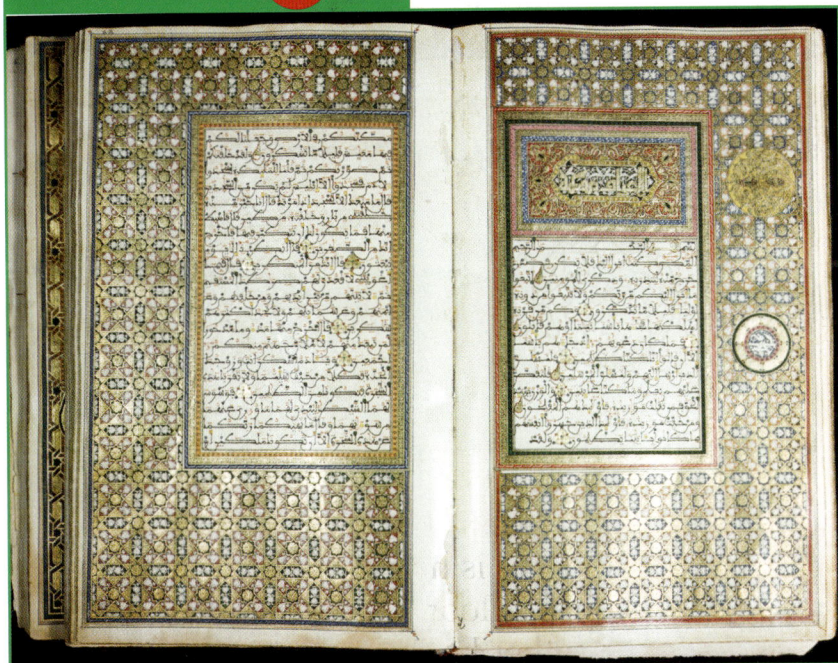

▲ *Pages from the Qur'an.*

SOURCE C

According to... who heard it from... who heard it from... who heard it from... who heard the Prophet say.

▲ *Every hadith starts with a record of how the story was passed down.*

Aisha

Aisha was the last wife of Muhammad.

1 She was much younger than him – she was 18 when he died (in 632) – and she lived until 678.

2 She was very clever and wise.

3 She collected 2,210 hadith.

4 Muslims believe she is one of the four most perfect women of all time.

5 She once went into battle for Islam, riding on a camel.

Tasks

1. How do **Sources A** and **B** show respect for the Qur'an?

2. Can you suggest reasons why Muslim children are made to memorise the Qur'an?

3. Why, do you think, does a hadith begin with a record of how the story was passed down? Why is this very useful for historians?

4. Aisha is sometimes called 'the Mother of All Believers'. With this in mind, choose what you think is the most important fact about her.

5. Tell the rest of the class the fact you have chosen, and explain to them why you think it is so important.

6. Do you think that people still need a strong faith in today's world?

Who should succeed the Prophet?

Your Mission: to work out what happened when Muhammad died.

When Muhammad died in 632, there was a lot of trouble about who would be the Caliphs (leaders) after him. If they were able to come back today, this is what the people from those times would have said:

1

Abu Bakr: I was Aisha's father, and became the first Caliph, but I was old and died after only two years.

2

Umar: I was the second Caliph – for 10 years. I was killed by a slave while I prayed.

3

Ali: I did not agree with what the Caliphs were doing. At first I said that I did not want to be Caliph.

4

Uthman: I became the third Caliph – for 12 years – but I was unpopular and was murdered.

5

Naila: I was Uthman's wife. My fingers were cut off trying to save him from the murderers. I blamed Ali for his murder, and I asked my nephew Muawiyya to help.

6

Ali: After Uthman's death I was the fourth Caliph – for five years. Muslims split between those who supported me and those who fought against me.

7

Aisha: I did not want Ali and fought against him.

8

Muawiyya: I blamed Ali for Uthman's murder. I asked for a meeting to decide who should be Caliph. When Ali was murdered I became the fifth Caliph – for 19 years.

9

Ali: I agreed to a meeting to decide who should be Caliph. It went badly. Then I was killed by some of my own men who said I should not have agreed to the meeting.

SOURCE **A**

How Ali was tricked

A meeting was held to hear both sides.   A man called Amr spoke for Muawiyya.   Abu Musa spoke for Ali.

Amr was clever.   'You go first,' he said to Abu Musa.   It was a trick so that he always could see what Abu Musa was up to, but Abu Musa agreed.

'Both men should stand down,' said Abu Musa, 'and we will let the people say who they want.'

'I agree,' said Amr.

Abu Musa went to the people.   'Both men will step down,' he told them.

Then Amr said: 'Abu Musa has said that Ali will step down, but Muawiyya won't – so he is the rightful Caliph!'

▲ *Written by an Arab historian about 900.*

Tasks

1.   Muhammad died in 632.   Using the information on these pages, work out:

● the order in which the five Caliphs came to power after him,

● what dates they ruled

and mark them onto the timeline you began on page 5.

2.   Can you think of any examples in the world where people are arguing or fighting about religion?   Do you know of any times in history when people have fought over religion?   Suggest reasons why people go to war for religion.

2 THE EMPIRE UNFURLS 632–1000

IN THIS CHAPTER YOU WILL LEARN:
- Why the Muslim Arab Empire grew so big.
- Why the Empire stopped growing.
- What life was like in Muslim Spain.

NEW WORDS

invaded

strength

weakened

Saracens: a Christian hate-word for the Muslims in the Middle Ages.

Shias: Muslims who believe Ali should have been Caliph.

Sunnis: Muslims who opposed Ali being Caliph.

Expansion and division
Under the first Caliphs, the Arab Empire grew quickly:

- Abu Bakr conquered the whole of Arabia.

5
- Umar took over the Persian Empire – AND invaded North Africa!

- Under Uthman, Muslim armies reached India.

Change
Caliph Muawiyya changed the way the empire
10 was run. He lived in Syria and ruled like a king. Also, he made sure that his son became Caliph after him – in the past, the Caliphs had been chosen by the people.

SOURCE A

▲ *The growth of the Arab Islamic Empire 600–750.*

Key
- Conquered in Muhammad's lifetime (to 630)
- Conquered by 656; Abbasids
- Conquered by 656; other Caliphs
- Conquered by 725; Al-Andalus

Muawiyya's family – the Umayyads – ruled for
15 90 years.   It was a good time for the Muslim
Empire.   Arab armies conquered Spain and
invaded France.   There was lots of trade and the
empire became rich.

The Abbasids

20 In **750** a Muslim named Abu al-Abbas invited all
the important Umayyads to a meal – and had
them killed.   Then he made himself Caliph.
    Abu al-Abbas's family – the Abbasids – ruled
for the next 500 years.

25 ● They did not conquer much land.

   ● They built a new capital city called Baghdad
   (in modern Iraq) which became a great place
   of learning.

Division

30 The empire was too big to be ruled by one ruler.
The Abbasid rulers could not keep all the power
for themselves.   Different rulers became
important in different parts of the empire, and
they began to call themselves 'caliphs' too.
35   Also, Islam split into Shia Muslims (supporters
of Ali – see pages 8–9) and Sunni Muslims (who
disagreed with Ali).   Even today, Shia and Sunni
Muslims disagree.

SOURCE B

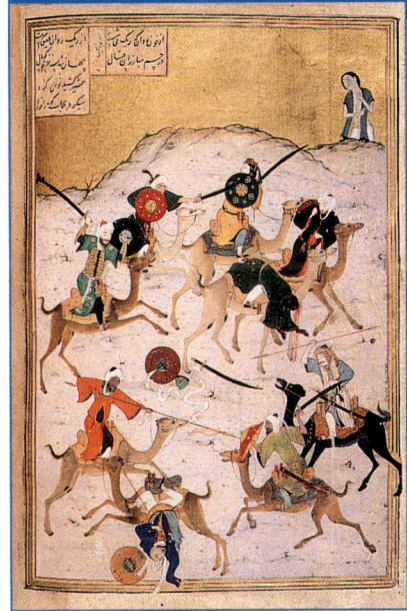

▲ The Arab armies used camels, which helped them win wars in the desert.

SOURCE C

Then the Christians said to the Muslims: 'Your rule is much better than the kings and rulers we used to have.'

▲ Written by a Muslim historian about 890.

SOURCE D

Arab soldiers were given the land they conquered.

   This – together with the belief that they were fighting for Allah – gave them a different kind of strength.

▲ Written by a modern Muslim historian.

SOURCE E

The Persian Empire was weakened by many years of war, and Constantinople was being attacked by tribes from northern Europe.

▲ Written by a modern historian.

Tasks

1. Add the date 750 to your timeline.

2. Read **Sources B–E**.   Find FIVE reasons why the Arab Empire grew so quickly.   List them in what you think is their order of importance.

11

The conquest of Spain

In 711 the Muslims invaded Spain and conquered it.

Muslim rule in Spain was a 'golden age' of riches and learning.

700: Spain is a Christian country, but the people hate their king, Roderick.

710: The Arabs have conquered all of North Africa. A Spanish noble, Julian, asks them to help him attack Roderick.

711: An army of 10,000 Muslims invades Spain.

750: Umayyad leader Abd al Rahman escapes being killed by Abu al-Abbas (see page 11). He flees to Spain and becomes ruler there, calling himself the Amir.

929: The Umayyad family in Spain start to call themselves 'Caliphs' of Al-Andalus.

950: The Christian kingdoms in the north of Spain begin to attack Al-Andalus.

NEW WORDS

amir: Arabic word meaning 'leader'.
noble: a lord.
revolt: rebellion.

712: More Arab armies invade Spain. Roderick is defeated and killed. Spain is conquered and called Al-Andalus. The Muslims invade France, but are defeated in 732.

SOURCE A

When Roderick was killed, the nobles of Spain asked the Muslims to promise not to harm their people or their churches.

In return, they promised to let the Muslims be their rulers, and to pay them taxes.

▲ *Written by a modern historian.*

SOURCE B

The Spanish people said that the new Muslim rulers were better than King Roderick.

▲ *Written by a modern historian.*

1086: The Muslims fight back, but after a while the Christians start attacking again, gradually re-conquering more and more land.

1492: The Christians finally conquer all of Spain and make the Muslims leave.

SOURCE C

The Muslims did not like France.

It was poor and backward, there was no trade, and the weather was awful.

▲ *Written by a modern historian.*

SOURCE D

What really stopped the Muslim invasion of France was a revolt by North African Muslims.

▲ *Written by a modern historian.*

Tasks

1. Add the dates 711, 950 and 1492 to your timeline.

2. Read **Sources A** and **B**. Why was it a good idea for the Muslims to leave the Christian religion alone?

3. What different reasons do **Sources C** and **D** give for the failure of the Muslim invasion of France?

What was Cordoba famous for?

The capital city of Al-Andalus was Cordoba. It was an amazing place. It became the largest city in Europe. It had running water and thousands of bath-houses.

New palace

The Muslim Caliphs built a huge palace – called the Madinat al Zahra – on a hill outside Cordoba. It took 40 years to build (936–976).

To visit the Caliph you had to walk down a 3-mile line of soldiers, and then go through a mile of rooms and huge halls, until you were shown into the Caliph's room – only to find him sitting in simple clothes, reading a book.

Books and writing

Cordoba had thousands of bookshops. The Caliphs built a library with 40,000 books – it had books by Ancient Greek writers that could not be found anywhere else in the world.

Cordoba was famous for its writers and musicians. Historians think that Muslim writers in Al-Andalus invented:

- Modern poetry – poems with short verses and lines which rhyme appeared for the first time in the part of France conquered by the Muslims.

- The novel – the first adventure books come from Spain.

NEW WORDS

palace, library, Ancient Greek musicians, poetry, rhyme, adventure novel, fashion, spices, courses, asparagus, deodorant, guitar
dyeing: colouring something.
mosque: a Muslim place of worship.

SOURCE A

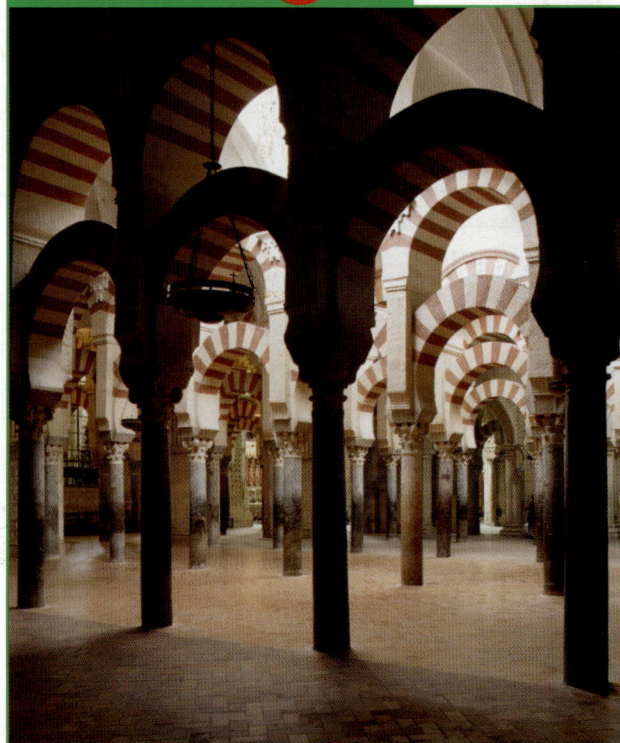

▲ *The Great Mosque of Cordoba. Now a Christian church, it is one of the biggest churches in the world.*

Fashion

Rich Cordobans drank from beautiful glasses, not metal mugs like the rest of Europe. They loved to try new foods and tasty spices. They wore flowing robes made out of fine colourful silks, not thick wool coats. And they loved fashion – for example, they painted their legs gold.

SOURCE B

▲ *Muslim and Christian musicians playing music together.*

Ziryab

Ziryab lived in Cordoba in 822. Here are some of things he made fashionable:

- A set order of courses in a meal.
- Tablecloths.
- Asparagus.
- Wearing different fashions in summer and winter.
- Hairdressing, and dyeing your hair.
- Deodorants.
- Toothpaste (and cleaning your teeth).
- Chess and polo.

SOURCE C

All the young Christians collect Arab books, and they say that Arab writers are the best in the world.

They write better Arab poetry than the Arabs!

The Muslims of Al-Andalus invented a kind of guitar!

▲ *Written by a Spanish Christian in 854.*

SOURCE D

It has more people. It has bigger markets and better mosques.

Its people are cleaner. It has more baths and hotels than anywhere on earth.

▲ *Written by a Muslim c. 950.*

Tasks

1. Add the Madinat al Zahra to your timeline.

2. Working with a partner, make a list of everything that made Muslim Cordoba amazing.

3. Write a rhyming poem with four-line verses about Cordoba.

How free and mixed was Al-Andalus?

Your Mission: to discover how multi-racial society was in Al-Andalus.

1. These slaves are from Africa and eastern Europe. The girls will go to Muslim homes as servants or dancers. The men will fight in the army. They will learn a little Arabic as time goes on.

(There are 14,000 slaves in Al-Andalus. They are not badly treated and have a right to see a doctor when they get old. Muslims cannot be slaves – a slave who becomes a Muslim must be set free.)

2. This noble comes from one of the Arab families who invaded Spain in 711. He speaks Arabic. His family were given good farmland and he pays no taxes.

3. This North African soldier is a convert to Islam. He speaks a little Arabic. He has some poor farmland and pays taxes.

9. These poor people are Spanish. They speak Spanish.

10. This Christian soldier has no land – his family's lands were given to the Arabs. He speaks Spanish and a little Arabic. He lives and dresses like an Arab and fights in the Muslim army.

11. This Jewish money-lender is very rich. He can worship as a Jew. He speaks Hebrew and Arabic. He is often called to speak to the Amir about money matters. Jews must wear yellow clothes to show they are not Muslims.

16

NEW WORDS

convert: to change to a different religion.

Arabic, Hebrew, Basque, inspector, treated

4.   A Muslim judge.

5. A Jewish market inspector.

6.   This Christian prince from the Basque area of north Spain is going to marry his daughter to a Muslim noble.   He speaks Basque and Arabic.   As a Christian, he is not allowed to ride a horse in Muslim countries.

7.   This woman poet has just come from Baghdad. She speaks Arabic.

8.   This visiting Christian trader is also rich.   He can worship as a Christian, and sell slaves.   He speaks French.
   (Jews and Christians can follow their own religion, but they have to pay taxes.)

Abd Al Rahman III
Caliph Abd al Rahman III's grandmother was a Spanish princess and his mother a Spanish slave.   His father was an Arab.   He had fair skin and dyed his red hair black to make himself look more like an Arab.

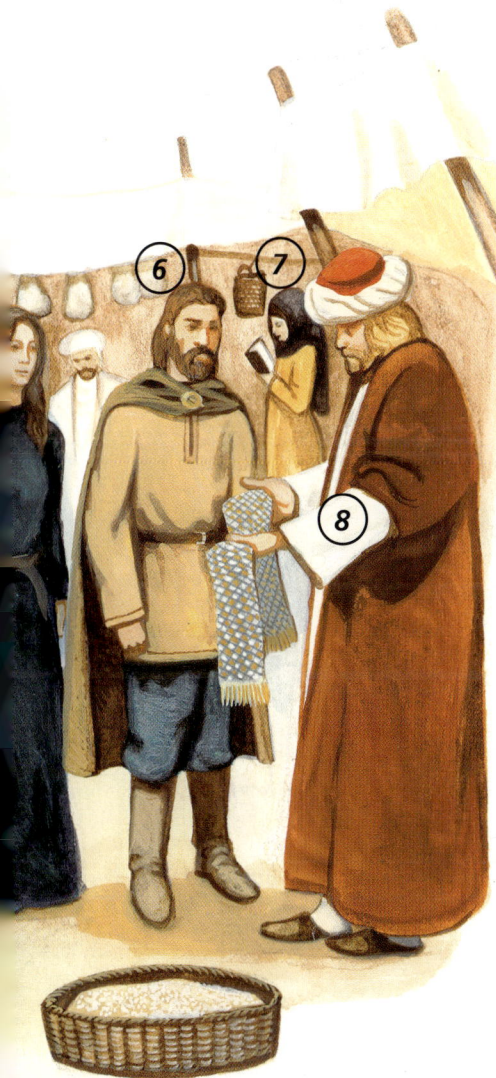

Tasks

1.   Use pages 16–17, to make a list of all the different races, classes and religions you can see in the picture.   Were they all treated equally?

2.   What principles should a multi-cultural society live by?   Was Al-Andalus a good multi-cultural society for everyone to live in?

Muslims believe that you must not force someone to believe in Allah.

THE BIG PICTURE

IN THIS CHAPTER YOU WILL LEARN:
- What the 'Five Pillars' of Muslim Society are.
- How Muslim society was organised.
- What life was like for women.
- What Muslim artists and scientists did.

NEW WORDS

pillar, treat, behaviour, divorce, punishments, messenger, execute

Sharia: Muslim law.

pilgrimage: a religious journey to a holy place.

fast: go without food to please God.

decorations, statues

muezzin: calls Muslims to prayer.

Imam: Muslim teacher.

Muslims believe that Muslims all over the world are united in a kind of family. They call the Islamic countries in the world 'The House of Peace'.

5   There are some things that ALL Muslims accept.

The word Sharia means 'the way to the oasis'.

What Muslims agree about

Islam is not just about what you believe – it is also about how you
10 treat other people. Muslim law is known as Sharia. It comes from:

- the Qur'an.

- things said by Muhammad.

- what Muslims think.

15 Sharia says that there are five kinds of behaviour:

- must do (e.g. pray)

- should do (e.g. free slaves)

- can do (e.g. be rich)

20 - shouldn't do (e.g. divorce)

- never do (e.g. drink wine).

Sharia has some harsh punishments, such as cutting the hands off people who steal, and
25 executing people for sleeping with somebody else's husband or wife.

The Five Pillars of Islam

Every Muslim accepts the Five
Pillars of Islam. This is how Islam
30 builds a strong and united religion
– all Muslims should:

a. believe in Allah, and
   Muhammad his messenger.

b. pray five times a day.

35 c. give money to the poor.

d. fast in the month of Ramadan.

e. go on a pilgrimage to Mecca
   once in their lifetime.

SOURCE A

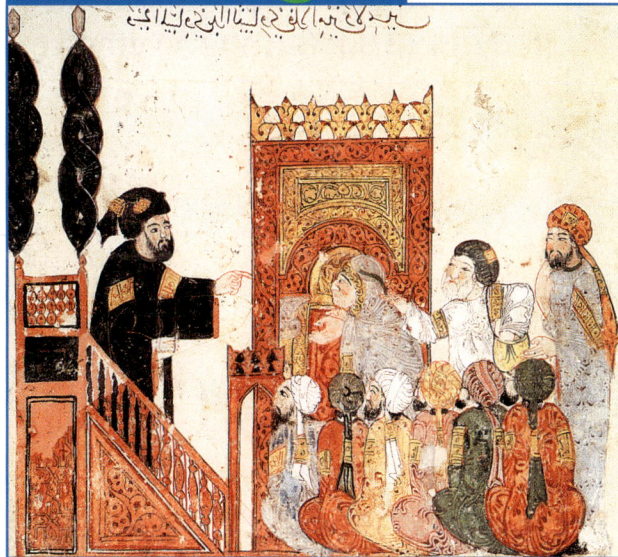

▲ *An imam talks to Muslims in a mosque.*

Mosques

Mosques are more or less the same   40
all over the world.

● A muezzin chants *Allahu Akhbar*
(meaning 'God is Great') to call
people to prayer.

● Inside there are prayer mats and   45
decorations, but no pictures or
statues.

● The men kneel down in lines
facing towards Mecca to pray.

● An imam gives a talk.   50

● There is a different area for
women.

Task

What 'musts', 'shoulds', 'cans',
'shouldn'ts' and 'nevers' do we
accept in our society today?
How do they compare with
Muslim law?

Social class

Muslims believed the same religion, but that didn't mean they were equal. In the empire there were many different classes of
5 people.

The ruling classes

The most important person was the Caliph. In the early years of the empire he was not just a religious
10 leader, he was leader of the government and the army as well. The Abbasid Caliphs were called 'The Shadow of God on earth'. To show how important they were,
15 they always took their vizier (adviser) and executioner with them.

In later times, the Caliph was more concerned with religion, and
20 a man called the sultan looked after the army and the government.

NEW WORDS

vizier: Caliph's adviser.

executioner: put criminals to death.

Sultan: ruler of the army and **government**.

warraqeen: booksellers.

related: in the same family.

The other classes

The least important people were the peasants who worked on the farms.
25

In between, there were many different groups. The richest were the great traders who traded all over the world. Also very important were the judges.
30

SOURCE A

▲ *Classes in the Islamic Empire. Can you spot the caliph, the vizier, the executioner, traders and soldiers?*

Other people in the middle classes were the craftspeople and shopkeepers, market inspectors, tax collectors and office workers.

35 One group that was very important were the warraqeen. They made paper, copied out books and sold them. Their shops were also meeting-places for teachers.

One Muslim writer counted 100 bookshops in one street in Baghdad.

40 Family was very important to the Muslims. Often people from the same family would live together in the same house, and related families in a city would try to live
45 near each other.

SOURCE B

The Caliph has all the power of a king, and he has all the power of religion, and this makes him very powerful.

▲ **Written by a Muslim historian.**

SOURCE C

The Muslims did not need a Parliament, because they trusted that their Caliph was a godly man.

▲ **Written by a modern historian.**

Tasks

1. Suggest reasons why the Caliph always took his executioner with him.

2. Read **Sources B** and **C**. How did religion add to the power of the Caliph?

3. Make a list of all the different classes of people you can find on pages 20–21, and arrange them in order of importance.

The life of women

Your Mission: to investigate the life of women in medieval Islam.

Were women badly treated in Islamic countries in the Middle Ages?

Law

The Qur'an says that men and women are equal
5 in the eyes of Allah. However, Sharia gives women fewer rights.
A daughter only got half of what a son got when their father
10 died. A man could divorce his wife by saying so three times, but a woman had to go to a judge.

15 ## Honour and respect

Women were respected, but they were not allowed to mix with men, or go on a journey without a man from her family with them.

Work and meeting people

NEW WORDS

marriages

births

Public Baths: in Muslim towns, a place where people could go to wash themselves.

SOURCE A

… you may marry two, three, or four [wives]….

▲ *From the Qur'an, Surah 4, Women, verse 3.*

SOURCE B

Muslim women have to cover their faces. In some Muslim countries they have to cover their whole bodies.

▲ *Written by an expert on Islam.*

SOURCE C

Most women worked. They were shopkeepers and craftworkers – they made most of the rugs and carpets.

Working women did not cover their faces.

▲ *Written by a modern historian.*

SOURCE D

Some women did have money of their own. They got it when their father died, or when they married, and some went into trade.

▲ *Written by a modern historian.*

SOURCE E

Rich women could meet each other on visits, at marriages and births, and on women-only days at the public baths.

▲ *Written by a modern historian.*

SOURCE F

▲ Noblewomen in a garden listening to Bayad, a popular singer and luteplayer.

Sex [20]

Islam teaches that wives must please their husbands, and that husbands must look after their wives – they must love each other. It tells Muslim men to marry a wife [25] who is religious, rich and pretty!

SOURCE G

Muhammad had nine wives.

▲ Hadith Sahih Bukhari, Book 62, Number 142.

SOURCE H

Love is an example of the wonderful things you will get when you go to heaven.

▲ Written by a Muslim about 1100.

Radiyya

Radiyya was the daughter of the Sultan of Delhi in Northern India. When her father died, her mother tried to kill her, but she took the throne and ruled for 4 years (1236–1240).

She:

● Won battles and conquered land.

● Wore men's clothes and rode elephants.

● Would not cover her face.

● Was overthrown when she let a man slave touch her.

Task

You are the friend of a Basque princess who is going to marry a Muslim noble (see page 17).

Work out a drama where she asks questions, and you tell her what to expect.   Try to include:

● What rights will she have?

● Will she be the only wife?

● How will she be treated?

● What she will be able to do/not do.

● How Muslims feel about love and marriage.

Cities, homes and gardens

A million people lived in Baghdad. Cordoba was almost as big.   London at the same time had less than 50,000 people.

Muslim cities were places of trade, news, plots,
5   learning, religion… and fun!   They had:

- Outside the city – market gardens, workshops and places where traders could leave their camels.   There was a wall round the city.

- Inside the city – different areas for different
10   tribes or for different kinds of shops.   Each area had its own mosque.

- In the centre – an open area called the madina. Also a bazaar (a market), a hospital and Islamic schools.

15 - On a hill outside the city there would be the army barracks and a palace, where all the government offices were.
The palace would be very beautiful and costly.

- Every Muslim city had to have green open
20   land without any buildings. Water was piped into the city to flush away the sewage.   Every
25   town had at least one public bath and a gym.

- Houses were built to keep the world
30   out.   The outside was a plain wall with screened windows.   Every house had a harem
35   (women's room).

SOURCE A

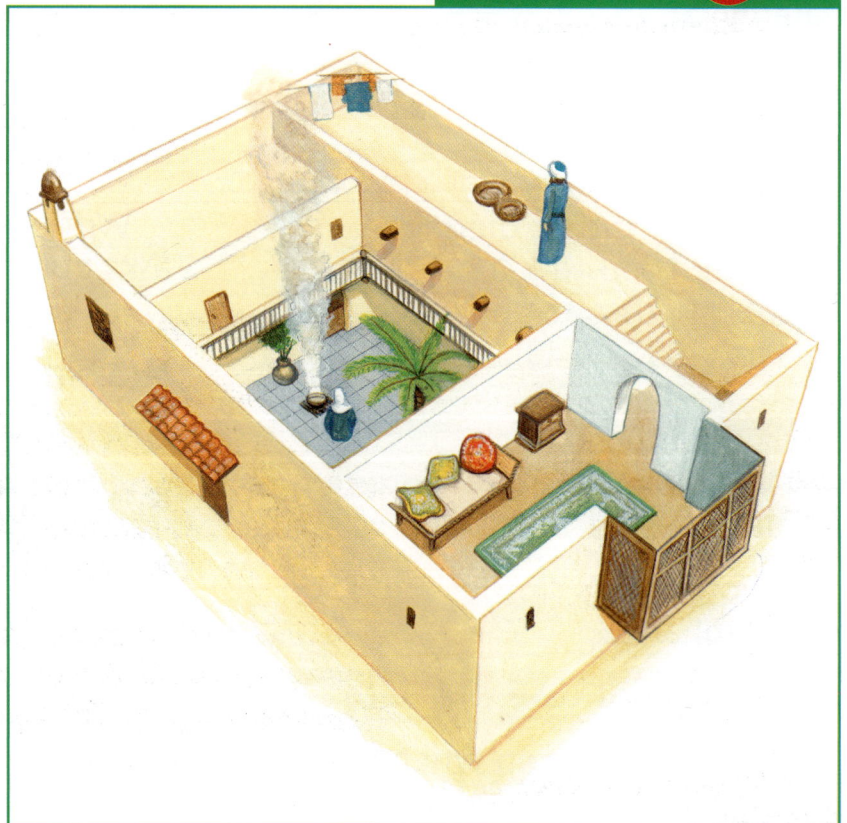

▶ A typical house in a Muslim city.

SOURCE B

A modern-day bazaar in Iran.

SOURCE C

House courtyard with garden. Muslims loved gardens. They said that heaven would be like a garden. The courtyard was where all the cooking was done. All the rooms were round the outside of this yard and opened onto it. There were few tables or chairs but lots of rugs, carpets and cushions.

The Arab word *dar as sina* (meaning a workshop) became the English word arsenal.

SOURCE D

Muslim cities were built around two centres – the market and the palace.

Written by a modern historian.

Tasks

1. Working with a partner, draw the layout of an imaginary Muslim city, marking onto it everything on pages 24–25. (Start by drawing a river and a hill.)

2. Using your plan, imagine you are a tourist going round the city. Trace out a route, and describe your 'visit' as excitedly as you can.

Islamic arts

Muslims love writing and books. They learn the Qur'an off by
5 heart. They also wrote poetry and stories about getting drunk and having a good time which were
10 very un-Islamic!

▲ 'Muslim artists made beautiful writing' – what shape does this writing make?

NEW WORDS

approve, trance, mistake
whirling Dervish: a dancing Sufi Muslim.

Muslim carpet-makers would always put a mistake in the pattern to remind people that only Allah is perfect.

◄ Mosques were often covered with amazing patterns and the words of the Qur'an.

Art

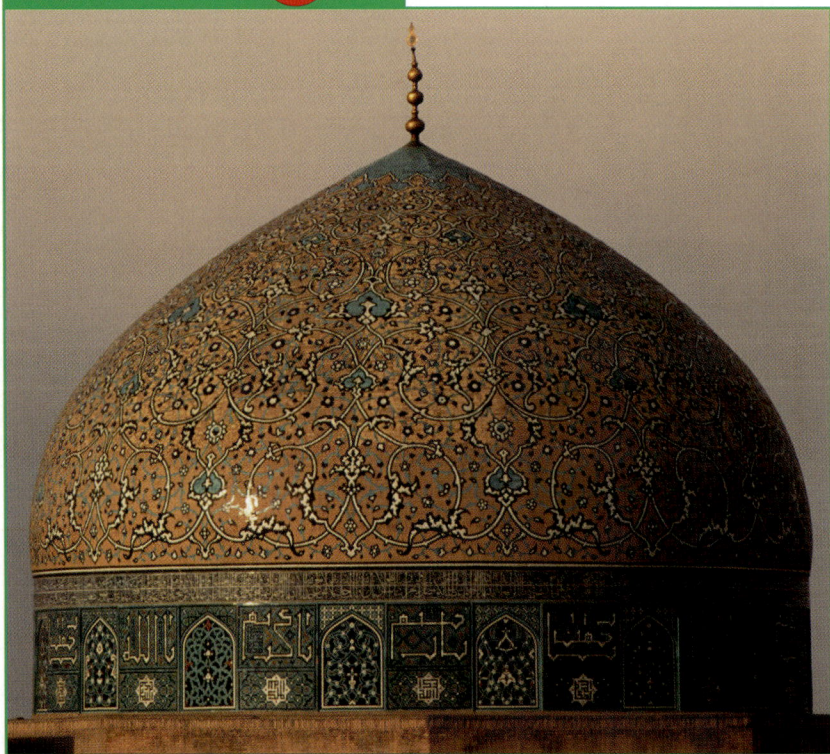

Islam teaches that it is wrong to draw people or make statues,
15 because only Allah should make the likeness of human beings. This is why, instead, medieval Muslim artists made
20 amazing patterns and beautiful writing.

This is also true about music and dancing. Muslims do not approve
25 of music and dancing. They say it puts 'evil thoughts' in people's minds. Dancing is not mentioned in the hadith, and music only once – when we are told that camels do not like it because they think they are going to be killed. And yet we know that Muslims in the Middle Ages LOVED music and dancing.

The 'whirling Dervishes' turned
35 round and round standing on one leg. This put them in a trance, which made them feel closer to Allah.

SOURCE C

▲ *Whirling dervishes, 1490.*

◄ *A party, with music and dancing, in a Muslim palace in 1600.*

SOURCE D

Tasks

1. Look at **Source B**. Find THREE different styles of decoration. Copy a bit of your favourite pattern.

2. Look at **Sources C** and **D**. How are they different? Suggest reasons why Muslims danced and sang when their religion said it was wrong.

3. Draw some of your own 'calligraphic animals' using English letters.

Islamic science and technology

Your Mission: to find out about Muslim science in the Middle Ages.

Muslim teachers made many advances in science and technology. Eventually their ideas reached Europe and started the modern world!

Here are their top ten advances:

5 **a.** Al-Khwarizmi (died 850) invented the idea of zero! This let him invent our modern system of tens and units. Before that, Roman numbers had been impossible to use – try to add MCCLIX to CIV and see how far you get! Without Al-Khwarizmi's maths, we would not today have been able to run businesses, build bridges, go into space or make computer chips.

b. Al-Battani (d. 929) worked out exactly how long a year is – important for modern
15 astronomers.

c. Al-Fazari (d. 790) invented the astrolabe – which told Muslims the time and the direction of Mecca, wherever they were in the world. It helped
20 sailors and traders.

d. Al-Haytham (d. 1039) realised that we see by light bouncing off things (we would never have invented television if he had not
25 discovered this!).

e. Caliph Muawiyya (d. 680) was said to be the first chemist. The word 'chemistry' comes from the Arab word Al Khemia.

30 **f.** Muslims used water-wheels – which were used in the Industrial Revolution, 500 years later.

SOURCE A

Roman numerals	Arabic numerals	Modern European numerals
	+	0
I	١	1
II	٢	2
III	٣	3
IV	٤	4
V	٥	5
VI	٦	6
VII	٧	7
VIII	٨	8
IX	٩	9
X	١+	10

SOURCE B

▲ *Muslim astronomers. A man at the back holds an astrolabe.*

g. Muslim doctors were much better than Christian doctors. Ibn Nafis (d. 1288) said that blood goes round the body 340 years before the English doctor William Harvey 'discovered' it. Baghdad had 60 hospitals at a time when there were none anywhere else in Europe.

Where would we be nowadays without hospitals?

h. Muslim sailors invented the triangular 'lateen' sail. This makes it possible to sail boats into the wind. Without it, Columbus would never have discovered America.

i. Muslims drew maps of the world they knew. Before this, Europeans had not known about places like India and China!

j. Muslims built the first university in the world, in Egypt in 970.

SOURCE C

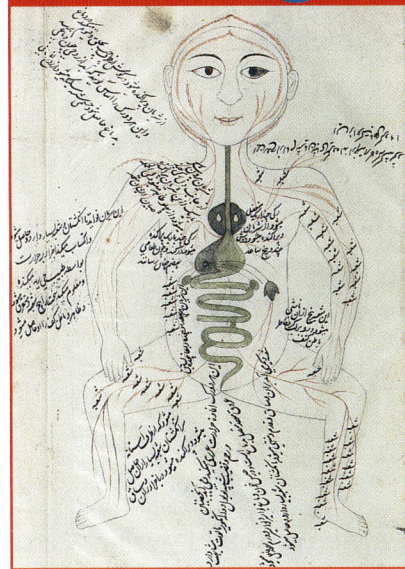

▲ *A Muslim drawing of the body.*

SOURCE D

▲ *A Muslim map of the world (turn it upside down!)*

Tasks

1. Add Al-Khwarizmi and Ibn Nafis to your timeline.

2. Working in a group:

a. Put the top TEN Muslim advances in order of importance.

b. Use your top FIVE to make a wall-chart: 'Muslims Made the Modern World'.

● On it put pictures or drawings of the FIVE advances, and pictures or drawings of the things they led to.

● Draw arrows to join the advances to their effects.

● Design your poster so it shows which advances were most important.

THE BIG PICTURE

IN THIS CHAPTER YOU WILL LEARN:
● The main invasions of the Muslim Empire.
● How important religion was in the Crusades.

NEW WORDS

Crusade: a war by Christians against the Muslims.

knights, sword, wrapped, trample

After 1000, the Muslim Empire was attacked by four waves of invaders.

Turkish Terror!

The Turks were from Asia. They
5 were great fighters. After 1040, they attacked the Muslim Empire. In **1055** they captured Baghdad.
They did not kill the Caliph, but they took all the power.

Al-Andalus Attacked

10 After 950, the Christians of northern Spain began to attack the Muslims of Al-Andalus.
Slowly, they re-conquered the whole of the country.
15 In 1492, the Christians conquered Granada (the last area held by the Muslims) and threw all the Muslims and Jews out of Spain.

SOURCE A

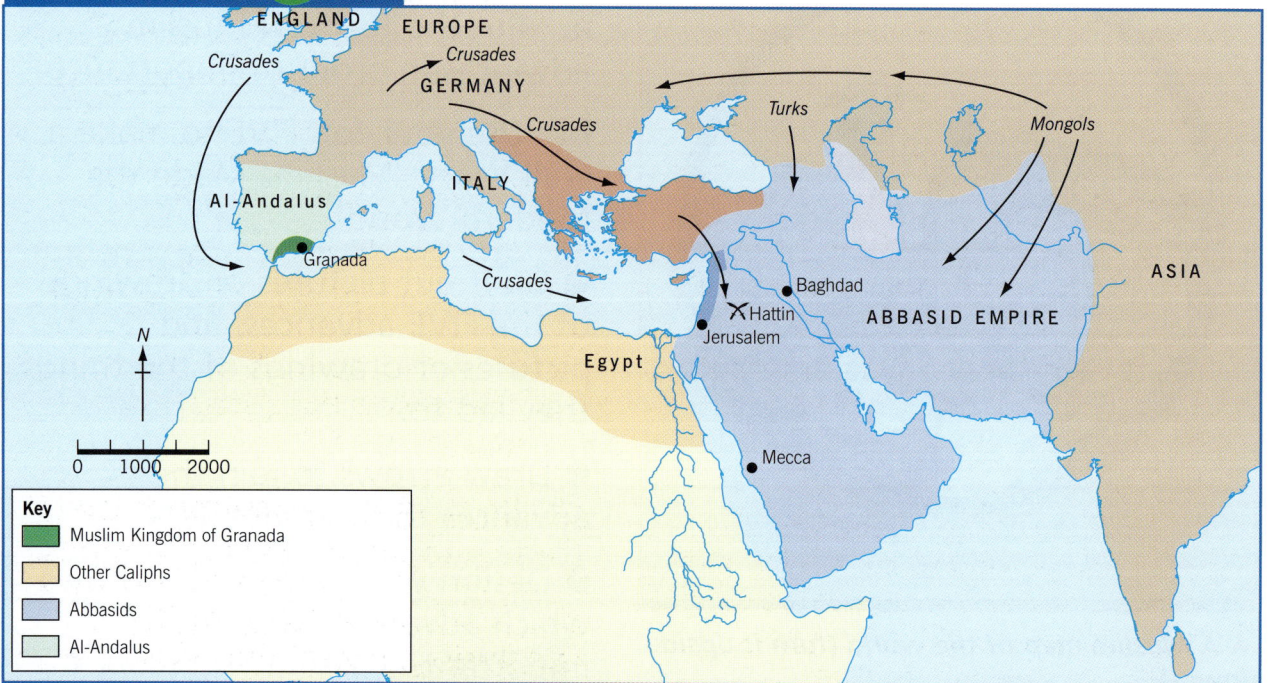

▲ *Attacks on the Islamic Empire, 950–1500.*

➤ *Genghis Khan (standing on the steps) tells the people of Baghdad that God has sent him to punish them.*

Genghis Khan ruled all the lands from China to the Black Sea. He probably ruled more land than any other person in history.

SOURCE B

20 # CRUEL CRUSADERS!

In 1095, the Pope asked the Christian knights of Europe to go to the Holy Land and drive the Muslims out of Jerusalem.

25 Between 1096 and 1300 there were eight Christian 'Crusades' to attack the Muslims, but they failed.

Mighty Mongols

The Mongols also attacked the
30 Muslim Empire. Genghis Khan (1167–1227) was a great soldier from Asia. First, he conquered China. Then he attacked the Muslim empire.
35 Genghis Khan died, but his grandson conquered Baghdad in **1258** and killed 800,000 people – and he even killed the cats and dogs.

The Mongols believed that it was wrong to kill a ruler with the sword, so they wrapped the Caliph in a blanket and let their horses trample him to death.

Tasks

1. Add the dates 1055, 1096 and 1258 to your timeline.

2. Using the facts and the four headlines on pages 30–31, design and write a newspaper front page reporting on the invasions *as if you were a Muslim writing about them.*

Write in newspaper style:

a. Start with a brief summary, then re-tell the story giving more details.

b. Use short, easy, exciting sentences.

c. Be biased! Remember that these people are killing Muslims.

d. Finish each story with a conclusion, explaining WHY.

Were the Crusades a Jihad?

Many people today are frightened by the idea that some Muslims may be waging a 'holy war' to conquer the world for Islam.

But, during the years 1096–1300, were they the
5 victims of a holy war *against* Islam?

This spread looks at the question: were the Crusades a holy war?

What started the Crusades off?

In 1095, Pope Urban gave a speech in France.
10 The Turks and Arabs, he told the people, had killed Christians, taken their lands and destroyed their churches. He asked all Christians 'to destroy that vile race'.

'Christ commands it,' he said.

15 ## Why is Jerusalem so important?

Jerusalem is the Holy City of the Christians, the Muslims and the Jews. The Christians who went on Crusade tried to conquer Jerusalem.

NEW WORDS

victims, commands, armour, waging, ambulance, suggested

holy war: a war for religion.

Holy City: Jerusalem.

vile: horrible/nasty.

sinners: people who do wrong things that anger God.

St John's Ambulance, which helps at events such as football matches, comes from the Order of St John – an order of fighting monks who fought in the Crusades.

SOURCE A

▲ *Jerusalem, the Holy City. The wall at the front is all that is left of the Jewish Temple. On the right is the Muslim Dome of the Rock mosque.*

SOURCE B

Kings wanted to conquer countries.

Traders wanted to make money.

Nobles wanted land. Soldiers wanted to fight.

And sinners wanted to earn a place in heaven.

▲ *Written by a modern historian.*

Were there other reasons for the Crusades?

20 On the face of things, therefore, it looks as though the Crusades were a religious war.

But historians have suggested many other reasons why people went to fight the Muslims. They say that some soldiers went to try to get

25 land, and others went just for the love of killing and stealing. Traders wanted to trade with the Muslim Empire – perhaps they joined the Crusades to make money? Did some people go just for adventure and to 'see the world'?

30 ## The Children's Crusade

The saddest crusade was probably the Children's Crusade in 1212, which is remembered in the story of the Pied Piper. Thousands of children left their homes in France and Germany,

35 believing that God would give them victory over the Muslims. Many got sick and died, and others were stolen and sold as slaves.

SOURCE C

The lands where you are going are much better than here, and you will be rich.

▲ *Said by a priest trying to get people to go on Crusade.*

SOURCE D

Soldiers! Now you can kill without going to hell!

Traders! Here is a chance to make money!

▲ *Said by a monk trying to get people to go on Crusade.*

SOURCE E

Men would not have gone all that way to fight in armour in such a hot land unless they thought God wanted it.

▲ *Said by a modern historian.*

SOURCE F

The Muslims did not think that the invaders were waging a religious war.

▲ *Written by a modern historian.*

Tasks

1. Look at pages 32–33 and make a list of all the evidence that suggests that the Crusades were a religious war.

2. List FOUR other reasons why people went on Crusade.

3. Make a list of all the different kinds of people who went on Crusade.

4. Explain what you think – were the Crusades religious wars?

How successful were the Crusades?

For European historians, the Crusades are very important wars. But Muslim historians do not see them as important – for them, the Turkish and Mongol invasions were
5 much more important.

Success

The First Crusade (1096–1099) was a success. The Crusaders captured Jerusalem. They killed all the Muslim men, women and children in the
10 city. They took over an area of land about the size of Wales.

Who were the Assassins?

The First Crusade succeeded because it took the Muslims by surprise. At the time there were
15 also a number of revolts in the Muslim Empire.

Also, at this time, a Muslim group called the Assassins were causing trouble for the Muslims by killing government leaders.

Defeat

20 A Second Crusade (1147–1149) failed to win any more land. Then a new Muslim leader, Salah ad Din, began to attack the Christians in the Holy Land. In 1187 he trapped
25 a Christian army in the desert. He cut off their water, then attacked and defeated them at the battle of Hattin. All the 15,000 soldiers were killed or sold as slaves.
30 Later that year, Salah ad Din took back Jerusalem.

Truce

A Third Crusade (1189–1192) set off to try to conquer Jerusalem again.
35 It was led by King Richard I of England and King Philip of France. When they got there, the two men argued and Philip went home.

NEW WORDS

surprise
ruined
weapons
nuisance
Assassin: member of a Muslim group which murdered people – this is where we get our word 'assassination'.

The word 'assassin' comes from the Arab word 'Hashishin' because the assassins smoked hashish (cannabis) before they attacked.

SOURCE A

Richard I watches Muslim prisoners being put to death.

40 Without the French, Richard was not strong enough to take Jerusalem.   So he made peace with Salah ad Din and went home.   The Crusade cost so much that England
45 was ruined for many years after.

Life in the Holy Land

There were many more Crusades in the years which followed, but they all failed.
50 Many Crusaders, however, decided to stay in the Holy Land. The weather was good.   They got land.   Trade was good.
    The Europeans were finally
55 thrown out in **1291**.

SOURCE B

Some Europeans have come to live among Muslims.   Some of them are good men.

▲ *Written by a Muslim soldier at the time of the Crusades.*

SOURCE C

We are doing lots of trade with the Italians.   They are selling us weapons, which is helping us against the Christians.

▲ *Written by Salah ad Din at the time of the Crusades.*

SOURCE D

The Crusades were a nuisance to the Muslims, but did not do any real harm. The Crusaders did not conquer any important city.

▲ *Written by a modern historian.*

SOURCE E

We were poor there, but God has made us rich here.   We had no land there, but have big farms here.   We were nothing there, but are important here.   Why should we go back, when life here is so good?

▲ *Written by a Christian at the time of the First Crusade.*

Tasks

1.   Add the date 1291 to your timeline.

2.   Using pages 32–35, find all the evidence you can that the Crusades were a failure.

3.   Find all the evidence you can that the Crusades did not really worry the Muslims.

Two commanders compared

Your Mission: to decide who was better – Richard or Salah ad Din.

NEW WORDS

ransom: a payment to get back someone who has been taken prisoner.

Richard, the Lionheart

Born to be king.

Rebelled twice against his own father, the king.

Kept fighting the Third Crusade, even when the French left him.

Got the Assassins to kill an enemy.

Once killed all the men, women and children of a town because Salah ad Din did not pay a ransom on time.

Used a big iron sword, so heavy it could smash through rock.

Suggested his sister should marry Salah ad Din (to help bring peace).

Captured on his way home – England had to pay a huge ransom to get him back. His wars ruined England.

Salah ad Din, the Upstart

Born poor.

Rebelled against his master, the Caliph of Egypt, and took power.

Had to put down Muslim revolts before he could attack the Crusaders.

The Assassins tried to kill him.

After the battle of Hattin, put the prisoners to death slowly so it would be more fun.

Killed the leader himself.

Used a thin, light sword of steel, so sharp it could cut silk.

When he heard that Richard was ill, he sent him fruit to help him get better.

Used all his money fighting and giving gifts to his friends.

SOURCE A

▲ *A Christian and a Muslim playing chess.*

SOURCE B

If they had each other's good points, Richard and Salah ad Din would be the greatest men in the world.

▲ *What a Bishop told Salah ad Din when Salah ad Din asked what he thought of Richard.*

SOURCE C

Salah ad Din was loved by his men. But he won because of the Crusaders' mistakes, not because he was a good fighter.

▲ *Written by a modern historian.*

Chess is a war game. The Crusaders learned it from the Muslims. The Persian words *Shah mat* mean 'the king is dead'. We say them in a game of chess when we say 'Checkmate!'

Tasks

1. Using pages 36–37, find all the ways in which Salah ad Din and Richard were different.

2. Find ways they were the same.

3. Divide into pairs. One of you pretend to be a Crusader, the other a Muslim soldier in Salah ad Din's army. Act out a debate about who was the better leader – argue as strongly as you can for your own man!

IN THIS CHAPTER YOU WILL LEARN:
● **Which new empires grew up after 1500.**
● **How Elizabeth I compared to Akbar.**

NEW WORDS

Shah: Persian word for king.
Ottoman: tribe of Turks who ruled a Muslim empire in Turkey and Europe.
Mughal: Muslim emperors of India.
Minaret: tower of a mosque.
magnificent, voyage

The Turkish and Mongol attacks on the Muslim Empire did not destroy it. The invaders became Muslims. Three new empires grew up and
5 they conquered even more land for Islam.

The Safavid Empire

In **1502**, a 16-year-old called Ismail became Shah (ruler) of Persia. He
10 was a great leader who built up a huge and rich empire. This empire is called the Safavid Empire (see map).

Ismail followed the Shia form of Islam, and he attacked and killed Sunni Muslims.

The Ottoman Empire

In **1453** the Ottoman Turks conquered Constantinople.
The Ottomans set up a powerful empire. Christian boys aged
20 between 8 and 15 were taken away to be soldiers in the Ottoman army. The Ottomans wanted trade with Europeans – Christian traders who

SOURCE A

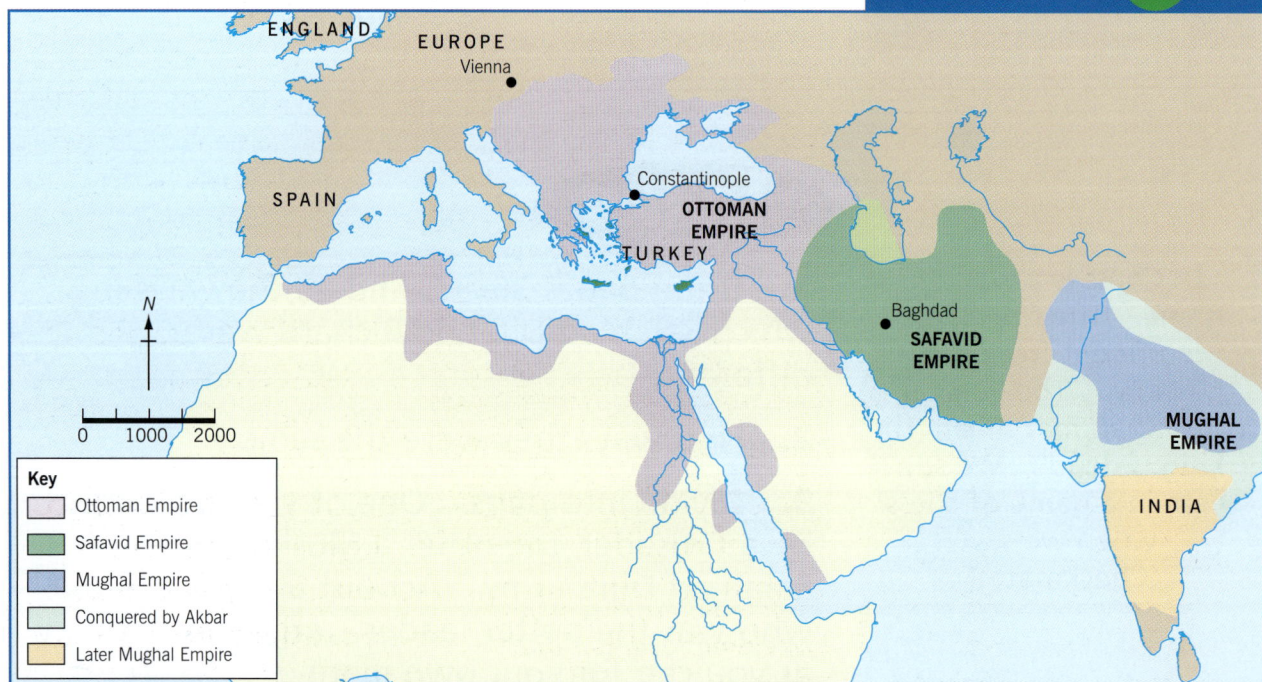

▲ *The Islamic Empires in 1700.*

Key
- Ottoman Empire
- Safavid Empire
- Mughal Empire
- Conquered by Akbar
- Later Mughal Empire

went to live in the empire could worship as Christians and have their own laws. But the Ottomans were also strict Muslims – any person who printed the Qur'an on a printing press was put to death.

The greatest Ottoman Sultan was Suleiman the Magnificent. He invaded eastern Europe and conquered lots of land. In **1529** his army got as far as Vienna before he was stopped.

The Mughals
The third Muslim empire was the Mughal Empire in India (see pages 40–43).

SOURCE B

Sea Voyages

1492 – Columbus sets off from Spain and discovers America.

1498 – Vasco da Gama from Portugal sails round Africa and reaches India.

1522 – del Cano returns to Portugal after 3 years at sea – the first sailing voyage round the world.

1580 – Francis Drake: first Englishman to sail round the world.

SOURCE C

▲ European ideas changed Muslim art.

SOURCE D

▲ Ottoman mosques have low domes and tall thin minarets.

Tasks

1. Add the dates 1502, 1453 and 1529 to your timeline.

2. Using an atlas, find out some of the countries of Europe which were in the past ruled by the Ottoman Turks.

3. Discuss pages 38–39 with a partner. Find TWO words which best describe the Safavid Empire, and the TWO words which best describe the Ottoman Empire.

The Mughal Empire

India had been strong, and the Mongols had not been able to conquer it.   But by 1500 India had split up into many weak
5   Muslim and Hindu states.

Babur was descended from Genghis Khan, and the word 'Mughal' comes from the name 'Mongols'.

SOURCE **A**

▲ *Babur's army used elephants to conquer India.*

Dynasty

In 1526 a Muslim called **Babur** (d. 1530) attacked India.   He set up an empire called the Mughal Empire.

Babur's son **Humayun** (d. 1556)   10
could not hold on to the new empire.   In 1540 he was defeated and had to flee to Persia.   He came back in 1555, but died soon after when he fell down some stairs on   15
the way to prayer.

Akbar

Humayun's son **Jalal** (d. 1605) was only 14 years old when he became emperor, but he grew up to be a   20
great ruler.   He made all of India part of the Mughal Empire.   He was so great that he was called Akbar (meaning 'the Great').

SOURCE B

▲ *Babur also had new weapons, including gunpowder.*

SOURCE C

The Mughal emperors built towers out of the heads of people they had killed.

▲ *Written by a modern historian.*

Fallout and murder

Akbar's son **Jahangir** (d. 1627) became the next emperor – although his wife was the real boss in the empire! When Jahangir died, his sons fought each other to become emperor. The winner was **Shahjahan** (d. 1666).

In 1658 Shahjahan fell ill. His son, Aurangzeb, murdered all his brothers and put his father in prison!

Aurangzeb (d. 1707) was a strict Muslim. He attacked the Hindus and made them pay extra taxes. His last years were spent fighting wars of religion against the Hindus.

Tasks

1. Add the following to your timeline:

● Babur conquers India,

● Akbar,

● Shahjahan.

2. How might new weapons (see **Sources A** and **B**) have helped the Mughal emperors to conquer India.

3. How might towers of heads (see **Source C**) have helped them?

4. Work out the list of Mughal emperors with the dates they reigned. Write a fact about each one.

What did the Mughals achieve?

Tolerance

The time of Akbar was a 'golden age' in Indian history. Akbar let Muslims and Hindus
5 worship in their own way, and tried to get them to understand each other.

Art and science

Akbar could not read and write,
10 but his reign was a time of learning.   During his reign Indian teachers wrote books on maths, science, medicine and astronomy.

Building projects

15 Akbar built wonderful palaces which were big and strong but covered with fancy stonework and decorations.   He also built beautiful gardens.

NEW WORDS

tolerance: allowing different ideas.
reign, harvest, starved, saint

The Taj Mahal

20 Akbar's grandson Shahjahan is famous as the man who built the Taj Mahal.   His wife died, and he built it to show how much he had loved her.
25

It took 20,000 workers 22 years to build (1632–1653).   He spent so much money on it that, when the harvest failed, he did not have enough money to buy food for the people and many people starved to death.
30

When Aurangzeb put Shahjahan in prison, he put him in a cell where he could just see the Taj Mahal.
35

SOURCE **A**

▲ *The Taj Mahal.*

SOURCE B

▶ *This drawing of St John, a Christian saint, is by the Muslim artist Abu'l Hasan, when he was just 12 years old! It copies European artists of the time.*

▲ *This drawing shows Babur building a garden.*

SOURCE C

▲ *Akbar built a new city called Fatehpur Sikri.*

SOURCE D

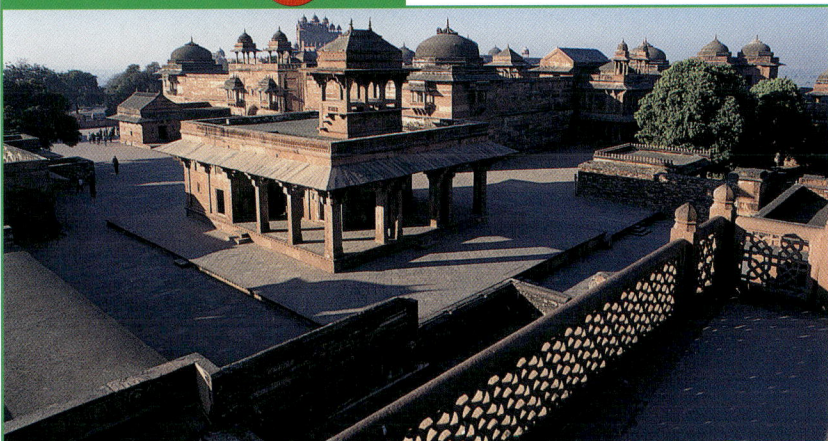

Tasks

1. Add the Taj Mahal to your timeline.

2. Study **Sources A–D**. Which source proves that the Mughals:

● loved art?

● loved gardens?

● learned things from Europeans?

● loved buildings?

● respected different religions?

43

Survival skills for rulers

Your Mission: to compare Akbar and Elizabeth I of England.

Both Akbar and Elizabeth I came to rule in a time of religious trouble and war, when their rule was in danger.

Akbar

5   **Born 1542.   Emperor from 1556 to 1605.**

- ● **Akbar was a great soldier.   He spent 90% of his taxes on the army.**

- ● **Akbar changed the way India was ruled.   He let clever people join the**
10   **government, not just nobles.   He set up government departments to run the country.**

SOURCE Ⓐ

▲ *A pencil drawing of Akbar (in a European style of art).*

- ● **Akbar allowed people to worship in their own way.   He was a Muslim, but**
15   **he married Hindu wives.   He tried to get Hindus and Muslims to understand each other.**

- ● **Every day, Akbar came to a window of his palace and waved to the people.   He liked to meet the people**
20   **and talk to them.**

His rule was a time of growth and success:

- • **Took power over all India.**

- • **Indians learned things from Europeans.**

- • **Buildings, books, art and gardens.**

△ *When Elizabeth was young, she was pretty. When she was older, she had black teeth and a spotty face. She wore thick white makeup and a red wig.*

Elizabeth was the greatest queen England has ever had.

△ *Written by a modern historian.*

Akbar tried to see the good in every man and race and religion. There was no one like him.

△ *Said by Jahangir, Akbar's son.*

Akbar's hobby was keeping pigeons.

25 **Elizabeth**

Born 1533.   Queen from 1558 to 1603.

● Elizabeth was in constant danger from Catholics,   She built up the English navy and defeated the Armada.

30 ● Elizabeth never married.   She let other rulers think they had a chance of marrying her so that they would not attack England.

● She tried to find a 'Middle Way' in
35 religion that all people could accept. But she executed people who plotted against her.

● She went round the country visiting different places.

40 Her reign was a time of growth and success:

• Francis Drake sailed round the world.

• English settlers landed in North America.

45 • Shakespeare wrote his plays.

Tasks

1. Using pages 44–45, find all the ways in which Akbar and Elizabeth were different.

2. Find ways they were the same.

3. Divide into pairs.   Choose a ruler each and debate who was the better ruler – argue as strongly as you can for your own choice!

Abbasids 11, 20
Assassins 34, 36
Arts 26–27, 39, 42, 43, 44
Crusades 31–37
Children's Crusade 33
Hattin, battle of 34, 36
Learning 11, 12, 24, 28–29, 42

Men
Abd al Rahman 12
Abd al Rahman III 17
Abu al-Abbas 11, 12
Abu Bakr 8, 10
Akbar 40, 42, 43, 44, 45
Al-Battani 28
Al-Farazi 28
Al-Haytham 28
Ali 8–9, 11
Al-Khwarizmi 28
Aurangzeb 41, 42
Babur 40–41, 43
Columbus 29, 39
Genghis Khan 31, 40
Humayun 40
Ibn Nafis 29
Ismail 38
Jahangir 41, 45
Jalal (see Akbar)
Mongols 31, 34, 38, 40
Muawiyya 8–9, 10, 28
Mughal Empire 39, 40–44
Muhammad 3, 4–5, 6, 7, 8, 18, 19, 23
Ottomans 38–39
Richard I 34–37
Salah ad Din 34–37
Shahjahan 41, 42
Suleiman the Magnificent 39
Umar 8, 10
Urban, Pope 32
Uthman 8, 10
Ziryab 15

Places
Baghdad 11, 17, 21, 24, 29, 30, 31
China 29, 31
Constantinople 2, 3, 11, 38

Cordoba 14–15, 24
Egypt 29, 36
France 2, 11, 13, 14, 32, 33, 34
Hejaz 3
India 23, 29, 39, 40–44
Jerusalem 31, 32, 34–35
Mecca 3, 4, 5, 19, 28
Medina 5
Persia 2, 3, 10, 11, 37, 38, 40
Quraish tribe 3, 5
Spain (al Andalus) 2, 11, 12–13, 14–15, 16–17, 30, 39

Religion
Christians 2, 3, 5, 11, 12–13, 15, 16–17, 29, 30–31, 32–35, 37, 38, 39, 43
Dervishes 27
Hadith 6–7, 23, 27
Hindus 40, 41, 42, 44
Islam 2, 5, 6–7, 11, 18–19, 23, 26–27, 32, 38
Jews 16, 17, 30
Kaaba 3, 4, 5
Qur'an 5, 6–7, 18, 22, 26, 39
Safavids 38
Sharia 18, 22
Shia 11, 38
Slaves 8, 16, 17, 18, 23, 33, 34
Social Classes 16–17, 20–21
Sunni 11, 38
Taj Mahal 42
Turks 30, 32, 34, 38
Umayyads 11, 12

Women
women's role 22–23
Aisha 7, 8
Elizabeth I 44
Khadija 4, 5
Naila 8
Radiyya 23

Our phrase 'So Long!', which we say to someone we are leaving, comes from the Arabic word *Salaam*! ('Peace').